unfolding love

poems for tender hearts

james kerti

Published by Indigo Bloom Press
An imprint of The Indigo Bloom LLC © 2025

Cover design by Alek Milosavljevic

Interior design by Mobeen Fazal

ISBN: 979-8-9993904-6-2

Printed in the United States of America

First Edition

Portland, Oregon

2025

"May I be the tiniest nail in the house of the universe, tiny but useful."

—Mary Oliver

Introduction

The first time I heard the crystal story, I was pacing around my cottage on a rainy night, half-listening to the storm and enjoying a phone date, while my cat Delilah—clearly unimpressed—followed me around, voicing her objections.

I was talking with someone new, a woman who lived a couple of hours from my tiny oceanside town. We talked for hours about family, spirituality, and what it means to be a tender person in a world that isn't always kind.

At one point, she said something I've carried with me ever since.

When she was a little girl, her mom told her that we all come into the world holding a bag of crystals. Some of them are broken. Our work in this life is to meet people, compare crystals, and reunite the fragments—because sometimes, another person holds a piece of what we need to feel whole.

She and I only spoke that once. Our paths overlapped for a single, brief moment.

But that story stayed with me—a beautiful, spiraling microcosm of a metaphor that is, itself, a crystal.

At the time, I had been focused on my own healing after leaving a long relationship.

I was just beginning to reach out again. Not to find someone to complete me—I already knew how that story ends. But to see what might still be possible inside love.

For most of my life, love felt like something I had to earn, like a fragile thread I held onto with the fear that I was someone people forgot to bring with them. I kept myself small to stay close.

And when love didn't take my outstretched hand, I believed it was my fault—my own not-enoughness.

Those beliefs lived in me—in relationships, friendships, family, work, and in all the connections I wanted to hold dear. They were amplified because I'm a person with a big, tender heart that feels everything: connection, longing, absence, grief.

Deep connections find me. And when they leave, they change me. But with intention and effort, my path toward love began to shift—not as a fixed destination I could plug into a maps app, but as a way of walking.

I learned how to honor who I am while also protecting the parts of me that deserve care. I've stumbled along the way. I've fallen, scraped my knees, and stood again—each time more rooted than before.

Slowly, I've come to trust the shape of my own heart.

The way forward has been lit by crystal lanterns. One step at a time.

And along the way, I've gathered so many crystals.

This book is a collection of them.

An offering for the tender-hearted.

It's for those who were called "old souls" as children and "too much" as adults—and who learned to make themselves smaller in order to fit.

While our paths are our own, we can still light lamps for one another and become lighthouses in the dark.

And sometimes, it's not about lighthouses. Maybe we just need a warm light in the corner while we cry in an otherwise dark room.

Life moves in spirals, especially for hearts like ours.

If even one of your crystals lives in these pages, I hope it finds its way back to you.

About This Book

First, this is a book of poems. You're welcome to read it however your heart and mind ask.

Skip around. Come back later. Start at the end and work backward if you need to. Ask a furry friend to pick a page. There's no correct order, no hidden key.

Do your thing. You don't need to read this note.

But if you're someone who finds it helpful to understand the full context—hi, neurodivergent friends!—or if you feel like there might be something important in this book, this part is for you.

Unfolding Love is shaped like a composition, organized in six emotional movements. Each one carries a different tone.

Some movements may feel tender. Others might feel sharper or quieter. The emotional rhythm shifts—that's part of the shape, too.

Each can stand alone, but together, they form a spiral.

If you're someone who feels things deeply, you might know what that's like—circling familiar aches or thoughts more than once. And if that's true for you, you may also know how lonely that can feel, especially when the world keeps urging you to move on.

This collection is meant to meet you where you are. Not to rush you or change how you feel, but to be a companion along the way.

You'll also notice that each poem begins with a short prelude—a breath before the poem itself. It helps set the tone.

If you choose to follow the shape this book offers, the emotional rhythm may feel familiar in a way that's hard to name.

This isn't a book that tries to teach anything, but it might help you notice something you already knew and had been struggling to accept—and perhaps feel a little less alone in that.

Program Notes

❧

I.   Embers and Echoes

For what still lingers.
Memory, resonance, and the warmth that hasn't gone out.

- Likeness 19
- The Stars 21
- Kansas City 23
- Starlit 25
- Scrimshaw 27
- Silhouette 31
- Dog-Eared 33
- Palmistry 35
- Remembrance 37
- old times 39
- Kindling 41

II.   The Burn and the Break

For the moments that cracked open.
Rupture, grief, and the clarity that comes after heat.

- Plum 49
- Divergence 51

- Riverbank 53
- Parallel Lines 55
- The Die 57
- Damona 59
- Extinguished 61
- Figments in Color 63
- 161 Days 65

III. Beneath the Ash

For the aftermath.
Hush, heaviness, and the slow breath of what remains.

- Words Are Water 71
- Falling 73
- Dear Doubt 75
- The Stout Black Cat 77
- The Question 79
- Unburdened Sky 81
- Reclamation 83
- What Can't Be Told 85

Interlude

A pause in between. Two voices speak across time—carrying memory, reflection, and resonance.

- Entre-Acte Reveries 88
- Entr-acte 90

IV. Flicker and Smoke

For what still glows.
Longing, half-light, and the shape of what might enter.

- Flicker 97
- Heavy Heart 99
- What the Roots Remember 101
- Heart Fell 103
- Six of Swords 105
- Hourglass 107
- Fireflies 109
- Heart Sound 111
- Right On Time 113

V. Becoming the Flame

For the fire that clarifies, not consumes.
Self-recognition, rootedness, and the act of rising.

- Out of the Ashes 119
- Ally 121
- Unburied 125
- Cathedral Heart 127
- Saving a Life 129
- Indivisible 131
- Vernacular 133
- Broken (Open) 135
- Not Yet 137

VI. Light That Stays

For the warmth that remains.
Integration, tenderness, and presence without demand.

- Someone New 143
- Yellow Brick 145
- The Crucible 147
- Luna 149
- Songs of Samhain 151
- Drumbeat 153

Wherever you begin, may the words meet you there.

I

Embers and Echoes

I.

Embers and Echoes

Some memories return without warning.

Not because you're trying to remember.

Just—something small opens the door.

You hear a laugh ringing out across a crowded room.

An out-of-the-way city gets mentioned in passing.

You catch the scent of a particular cologne or perfume drifting through the grocery store.

You weren't looking for it.

But there it is: that ache you promised yourself you'd left in your yesterdays.

For a few seconds—or longer—your body holds something your mind can't explain.

Maybe it feels like a heaviness in your chest, or a pull toward something that no longer has a name—or remembers yours. There could be a sense that what you felt is still somewhere in you, waiting.

It doesn't have to mean you're stuck. It could mean something mattered and that a part of you is still listening even if you don't know exactly what for.

The poems that follow are made of that kind of moment—the ones that hum beneath the surface.

This isn't about being loud or dramatic. Just present.

The book I've gifted to more people than any other is Dr. Kristin Neff's *Self-Compassion*—because giving ourselves the caring support we'd offer a friend is at the heart of honoring our own tenderness.

If you're someone who tends to feel things deeply, you're probably used to being told to *stop* feeling the way you do.

As you read these poems, I'd like to gently encourage you: you don't need to do that.

Because the people and places we still carry—the embers and echoes we didn't mean to hold onto—maybe there's wisdom in them.

Though they might not hold the answers you once wished they did, they may still have something to show you.

Prelude to Likeness

Some moments aren't meant
to be explained, only noticed.

Something flickers. Someone resembles.
A part of you leans forward,
then thinks better of it. These are the maybes
that visit us like birds—never nesting
but stirring something all the same.

Likeness

From a Zoom crowd,
a face brushes
against something open—
a resemblance not exact,
but enough to stir
a thin-winged maybe
of something unwritten,
a chord I almost knew
how to play.
I look away
before the song starts
singing itself.

Prelude to The Stars

Some memories don't fade.
They just travel farther away.

They stretch into the sky,
waiting to be glimpsed again
when the world grows dark enough.

The Stars

We'll always have the stars
to remind us of what once was.

A skyward glance on a clear night
and I'm right back there with you:

easy evening words by the seaside spiraling
into giggle fits infinite as the twinkles above,

gazes held with no effort to find
words to match their meaning,

moments suspended in the salt air as our feet
bless the ground with fading footsteps.

One day
centuries from now

an astronomer on a distant star
will look upon our light.

Prelude to Kansas City

Some places become shorthand
for everything we don't say out loud.

A city, a street, a single name—and suddenly,
the air shifts. You're not there,
but a version of you is.
Maybe a version of someone else, too.

There are moments that beam toward you
from the past—not to pull you back,
but to remind you something mattered.

Kansas City

When someone tells me they're
from Kansas City, my heart skips
back on beat: diamond
daydreams, rainbow roads,
remembered melody. I wonder if
my ghost greets you
as warmly as your
echo beams at me.

Prelude to Starlit

Certain selves awaken only
in the presence of someone
who sees us with more than eyes,
and who doesn't try to fix
or shape us—only to meet us.

Starlit

We let the starlight and sea sound
shepherd us home. Not a house on a hill
but where our bigger selves dwell

and await a witness. They sit silently until
called to rise and speak at last,
reveal what was hidden, and surrender what is past.

Prelude to Scrimshaw

There's something about not knowing
how the story will end,
and whether it will last,
that invites a kind of presence
we rarely allow ourselves.
And that's what lets us
live those moments so fully.

Not everything beautiful endures.
But some things leave a mark
because we were there
for them completely.

Scrimshaw

We are there,
in those twilit times:
the sun sinking slowly seaward,
lost for the day,

home lights blinking on
in silent succession, then reversing
course as darkness makes
its home.

We dive
into the dead
of night, and deeper, deeper
into the depths

of what we are,
probing possibilities
of what could be.
Eventually. Maybe.

Perfect presence,
time impossibly
well-spent,
hours, minutes, seconds carved

into bone
with care
in a script
only we could read.

I can still hear
these familiar runes whispering
in a dead language
across the years.

Prelude to Silhouette

There will be times when caring
in the midst of uncertainty
is the most human thing you can do.

You don't have to wait for clarity
in order to hold something
or someone with tenderness.
Your presence can be sacred all on its own.

Silhouette

I see your shape through
February-frosted glass—
outline familiar,
details blurred.
Breath fogs,
then fades again.
No way to know
if you're turning
toward me
or away.

Prelude to Dog-Eared

Some things call us back
to a moment
before knowing, before clarity,
when all we can do
is reach and see
if something still responds.

Dog-Eared

Repeated prayers brought you near
a bound and beaten tome. Within your grasp,
a dog-eared page peeks out beside the copper clasp,
holding stories you've come to fear.

Your chipped nails point pageward,
searching for a missing sentence,
but reach too-late repentance
for the lost dreams of a caged bird.

Then, with trembling hands, you may find
on turned paper, faded ink, long since dried
on stories lived, with endings tied—
or shining space, waiting lined.

Prelude to Palmistry

Not everything holy arrives with wholeness.
But sometimes, just a touch is enough
to wake something dormant.

Palmistry

Your fingers traced a map on my palms,
lines never fully followed,
humming unraised into psalms—
truth only between breaths swallowed
into silence, never quite loud enough to echo.
Your touch paused at prophecy,
never practiced audibly.

Prelude to Remembrance

If you've ever felt like you had to shrink
to fit a world that didn't know how to hold you.

Remembrance

You—yes, you—from the Land of Big Feelings,
plunked down into this unfamiliar place,
clutter and clamor, wholeness and healings,
swirling, swept up in an unceasing chase
whose beginning lies beyond your recall:
Be still, and remember. You're big. Not small.

Prelude to Old Times

*This piece is about seeing someone again
after you've both become strangers.*

old times

i walked alone
for many years
since we last met
i lived many lives
i carried torches
i did not understand
now here we are again
you look different
let us talk about old times
without remembering

Prelude to Kindling

There are times when we can't understand
what something meant
until we feel the warmth it left behind.

Like reading an old journal and realizing
you were already carrying the truth.

Kindling

We burned our love for warmth
during a winter wandering up north.
In its splintering glimmer, we found
smoky memories of a seaside town:
late breakfasts, afternoon drives
drenched in quiet joy and loud smiles.

The fire's gone now.
And last May, that inn burned down.
But in the hush that followed,
I heard, on the wind, a sorrowed
crackling woven with triumphant cries—
the still-hot ashes of something that won't die.

II

The Burn and the Break

II.

The Burn and the Break

I think often about one of my favorite books, Donald Miller's *A Million Miles in a Thousand Years*. In it, he shares the process of working with movie producers to turn his popular memoir into a screenplay.

At one point, Miller questions the producers about why the protagonist couldn't just do the thing the author wanted him to do. They explained that for a character to make a real change, something—an "inciting incident"—needs to happen to spur them into action.

Miller's book is about how he used insights like this to make meaningful changes in his own life. It's a great read. But this one story stayed with me the most—because some truths only reveal themselves in the fire.

Not because they need light to be seen, but because there's something about the alchemy of flame that strips away illusion.

And when you've been holding a kind of love that's not meant to stay in the way you once hoped, you may need that fire to show you what's true—not before, but now.

Because not all changes are loud. Love may leave or shift without you noticing at first—half-shared glances, unanswered texts— until suddenly, you realize you've been carrying the weight alone.

And then what once offered steady warmth begins to scorch.

Or sometimes, the choice isn't made for you. It waits for you to hear your own heart whispering that—no matter how much you may want to—this place is no longer one you can stay in.

Either way, you're left to live with what was real—and what remains.

Those may be the same thing. But not always. Not always.

There is grief in the pages that follow, yes—but not the kind that asks for pity. And not the kind that asks you to shrink.

This grief stands tall. Shoulders back, head high. Bearing witness to what cracked open and could not be kept.

Grief is personal. And it often makes us feel alone.

That's why poetry matters here: poems don't demand specificity.

They make room for your own shape.

And these poems carry no blame. Only the burn.

Fire itself has no ill intent.

These words hold a lantern to the clarity that can only come after the smoke clears—patiently, because grief is not linear.

It loops.

It lingers.

Grief becomes a repeat visitor, like a popular song you can't avoid but that always takes you back to a tender memory.

This grief doesn't ask for anything. It just wants to be acknowledged.

Your job isn't to banish it forever. It's to let it be a quiet passenger rather than the driver.

But that doesn't happen by refusing it a seat in the car.

So, let's go for a ride.

No need to be alone.

Prelude to Plum

You knew what you gave.

Plum

You tucked your heart in a velvet purple bag
and held it out for them to take it.

When they asked what was inside,
you said, "Only everything."

They admired the plum hue
and walked away.

Prelude to Divergence

The wind doesn't ask for permission
before it changes direction.

Divergence

A love will come as wind will blow,
not to stay, though you may wish it so,
swept along by life's long hidden flow,
led by forces greater than you know.

Side by side, you walk and take it slow.
The seasons shift, and still, you grow.
But when paths diverge, you must let go,
carrying the lessons they bestow.

Prelude to Riverbank

*Just because you're no longer
walking beside them
doesn't mean you've stopped
listening for their footsteps.*

Riverbank

They say when you're lost,
you follow the river. And so our abandoned
waterside picnic gave way to glances
stolen at one another across
the distance now flowing and growing
between us with each diverging
step. The landscape shifted from verdant
to weathered to lush again, as we walked part
apart and partially together,
separate but not yet separated.
We repeatedly fell out of sight. Night
after night brought skyward wonder above
blanketing blackness, as you and I wondered
whether a familiar face would
share dawn's greeting, hoping
with a heart heavy with longing
long since turned to gratitude for
a companion, unseen, finding their way home.

Prelude to Parallel Lines

Some distances never grow wider.
They just stay beside you.

Parallel Lines

I've traveled the world searching
for words that might describe
the you who continues to live
a parallel life in my heart.

Prelude to The Die

It's already in motion.

The Die

The die is cast
now we clearly see
all that could not last
and moves to was from be.

Prelude to Damona

Sometimes, the memory doesn't knock.
It just walks in like it still has a key.

Damona

People arrived from leagues away
to drink my sacred waters and say
the old words their ancestors had spoken.

It feels like just yesterday
they stopped to worship before going on their way,
but the years passed hard, the cycle long broken.

I hear all the gnarled words today:
sewer, filth—their price, but I pay.
In this broken bargain, I've become just a token.

I've felt every season, every moon, every day,
each with their own song, since faded to gray,
so still I wait, solemn and oaken.

They knew it was mine, from river to bay,
and though they forget, I still hold much sway.
Even a poisoned goddess can one day be awoken.

Prelude to Extinguished

Some teachings are given with love,
but still leave us in the dark.

Extinguished

When I was a child,
my mother said: fill your heart
with goodness.

Holy words. Blessings.

She said they'd be like a fire
keeping the wolves away.

I did as she said.
For years.

Moths gathered like pilgrims
while howls rose
in the moonlit woods.

And my flame went out.

Prelude to Figments in Color

Some feelings don't insist on being spoken.
But they still need a place to go.

Figments in Color

I can't do this anymore.
Words run together like pigments
mixed for the picture I painted you before.
I sent silent notes to you—figments
of feeling, brushed in truth.
I wish the gentlest made it through.
Do you see me spilling past the seams—
too much to carry, too much for dreams?
I want—I won't,
I won't ever let it show,
but I still want you close.
(Even if I never say it aloud.)

Prelude to 161 Days

There are losses we understand
long before we're able to accept them.

161 Days

There's still a part of me, all these months gone by,
that thinks maybe I'll once again see you in life,
that our story didn't end that day in July.
No matter how much I try to tell myself otherwise
it eludes me. Even when I bathe in the truth, it can't sink inside,
like a wrung-out dish rag, never fully dry
in the same lonely spot. I cry and cry
as if I get it, then feel it's all a lie, a lie
that I won't see you again—and I don't know why
I still call out for you sometimes and anticipate your reply,
even as we had our last moments together, said goodbye.
I know if you could be here, you would—you were never shy
to tell me how you felt, with that goofy look and wry
smile of yours that endure—my bittersweet lullaby.

III

Beneath the Ash

III.

Beneath the Ash

You might be hoping for peace after the fire finally burns out. But it's not time for that yet.

First, there's a hush—after the walls of the house you'd been living in come crumbling down.

In this thick quiet, meaning hasn't emerged, but pain has stopped announcing itself—like a child in the backseat finally, mercifully falling asleep after hours of asking, "Are we there yet?"

It's not time to rebuild.

Not yet.

For now, it means sitting in the smoke, remembering how to breathe without pain.

Slow breaths and small questions become your companions here.

Comedian-violist Isabel Hagen has this brilliant bit about how love is the only thing that, after you lose it, makes you doubt whether it ever existed in the first place.

"No one ever loses their keys," she says, "and then they're like, 'Well, maybe there never were any keys?'"

You hear that joke and laugh. Maybe you wince a little.

Because you've done that, haven't you—doubted what you know you once held?

So now we enter the part of the book that comes after the flame has gone out, where grief is softer but no less honest.

This smoky grief gathers in corners and clings to your clothing like a spiderweb you accidentally walked into.

It arrives like a prayer that sounds more like a question—one you don't need to answer.

It's tempting to reach for solutions the moment the fire cools, when you finally think your heart is safe enough to be touched.

But know this...

This isn't a test.

No one's watching you, holding up a stopwatch, glancing over at other people's times.

You are right on time.

For you.

You're sitting at the edge of what's left with enough tenderness to feel what's real—and the strength to stay with yourself.

Prelude to Words Are Water

There's no right pace for language to return.
Some days, you dry up.
Some days, you overflow.

Words Are Water

Words are water. You can
contain but not grasp them,
and your glass only holds so much.

An even flow,
day after day,
then released again.

A babbling brook,
like a child full of secrets,
heard more than seen.

Forced through cracks in stone,
erupting as a geyser
or emerging a mere trickle.

A cleansing torrent
washing it all away.
You may need a bigger cup.

Prelude to Falling

Sometimes, there's nothing left to hold
but the unsteady belief
that you won't lose yourself
on the way down.

Falling

You fall
forward
joyously
jumping
into the well
of yourself,
where you find
pieces of you
tucked away
for a rainy day
that finally came
after many years.

Left with nothing
but the choice—
to trust.

So here you go,
because you must,
no landing
guaranteed,
nothing
to break your fall

nor you.

Prelude to Dear Doubt

Our oldest companions
may be ones we're never meant to name.

Dear Doubt

Dear doubt, welcome
back. I've missed the scent
of your clover cloak,
and your ancestral touch,
returning me to all the places
we used to visit together,

when you were old,
and I was young—

when we played in the stream
and chased butterflies,

when we hid in the closet
as chaos reigned around us,

when we went hungry
for refusing what was given,

and when we learned
the difference between

what love is
and what it only resembles.

Thank you, dear friend,
for walking me home,
and reminding me that
no matter how far I've come,
I am also who I've always been.

Prelude to The Stout Black Cat

Not every guide arrives with answers.
Some just stare until you remember.

The Stout Black Cat

The stout
black cat slips through dreams,
appearing when you doubt
the buried beams

bearing life's throes.
So you may rest,
and remember those
truths impressed—
like fingerprints laid
in the soul's deep fold—
signs that never fade,
silent and bold.

For long before its black eyes bore
into you with recognition,
there waited, deep at the core,
an ancient commission.

Prelude to The Question

There are questions that don't want answers.
They just want to sit beside your heart
long enough for you to feel them.

The Question

to be-
autifully break
or not to be-
autifully break

that is the question
of the open heart that lives
in the space

of your life's seasons
with rhyme or reason
but rarely both

and the only way
to answer is
by closing your heart

Prelude to Unburdened Sky

There are times when the weight lifts slowly.
And at other times, you may look up
and realize it's already gone.

Unburdened Sky

Let time when it's time.

Words that found me
through an autumn seaside fog
three dozen moons ago
cross a smoky land
and carry me
into sky
unburdened,
blue
without end

Prelude to Reclamation

Sometimes, it's not about brokenness
or wholeness, but finding it in you
to begin again either way—
not with what you lost,
but with what you choose to build.

Reclamation

She built her home
after the old building burned.
He was an arsonist.

From feathery ash and flaky dust,
made anew from what she learned
about self-trust.

A fresh purpose for every room,
past pains churned
into a bright spring bloom.

Musty carpets traded for shiny floors.
Walls adorned with creations returned
from long before.

Brick by brick, piece by piece,
each one hard-earned,
her place of power and ease.

Prelude to What Can't Be Told

Some things can only be carried
when your hands become ready.

What Can't Be Told

You could be me.
I remember being you.

Fragile futures bind
us for now, strings
of time threading needles,
like wizened hands
that have sewn
stories into seams
for generations.

If I warned of wintry, winding
mountain roads and cliffside
gusts from the north that battered
my frozen face for nights
beyond counting,
would you change course,
before realizing these directions
only hold meaning while
our shoes share footsteps?

Interlude

When the pain settles, you may begin to hear something gentler—an echo that lingers, as if your bones were struck like a tuning fork.

And if you listen carefully, you may sense a resonance that's different from what came before.

That's because it's only after the sharpest grief has stilled that you can sit in the soft space where memory hums without hurting.

So you sit, and listen, and feel.

Poetry can be such a good friend during those times.

Ella Wheeler Wilcox (1850–1919) is a poet whose work has long spoken to something tender in me.

Her poem Entre-Acte Reveries gave shape to a kind of shift I recognized—a reflective space between who I've been and who I'm still becoming. Both still true. Both still here. Just... something held differently now, as time keeps moving on.

My poem Entr'acte (after Ella) was written in conversation with hers. It carries the ache of not knowing what's next and the courage it takes to stay present in that pause, trusting that something new may still begin.

Together, they dwell in that tuning fork space.

Not quite past. Not quite future. Something in between.

Maybe it's a place to remember the beauty that once was—and to wonder what the music might sound like when it dares to return.

Entre-Acte Reveries
by Ella Wheeler Wilcox

Between the acts while the orchestra played
That sweet old waltz with the lilting measure,
I drifted away to a dear dead day,
When the dance, for me, was the sum of all pleasure;
When my veins were rife with the fever of life,
When hope ran high as an inswept ocean,
And my heart's great gladness was almost madness,
As I floated off to the music's motion.

How little I cared for the world outside!
How little I cared for the dull day after!
The thought of trouble went up like a bubble,
And burst in a sparkle of mirthful laughter,
Oh! and the beat of it, oh! and the sweet of it—
Melody, motion, and young blood melted;
The dancers swaying, the players playing,
The air song-deluged and music-pelted.

I knew no weariness, no, not I—
My step was as light as the waving grasses
That flutter with ease on the strong-armed breeze,
As it waltzes over the wild morasses.
Life was all sound and swing; youth was a perfect thing;
Night was the goddess of satisfaction.
Oh, how I tripped away, right to the edge of day!
Joy lay in motion, and rest lay in action.

I dance no more on the music's wave,
I yield no more to its wildering power,
That time has flown like a rose that is blown,
Yet life is a garden forever in flower.
Though storms of tears have watered the years,
Between to-day and the day departed,
Though trials have met me, and grief's waves wet me,
And I have been tired and trouble-hearted.

Though under the sod of a wee green grave,
A great, sweet hope in darkness perished,
Yet life, to my thinking, is a cup worth drinking,
A gift to be glad of, and loved, and cherished.
There is deeper pleasure in the slower measure
That Time's grand orchestra now is playing.
Its mellowed minor is sadder but finer,
And life grows daily more worth the living.

Entr-acte
after Ella

Who are you, sweet stranger, in the dark?
Once, you knew your face by reflection
in emerald eyes, your flickering spark.
Who are you now, untethered from that connection?

When the music fades and you sit alone,
do you find yourself praying for a sign
in the hush of reserved seats and arching stone,
or asking in silence: *why that path, not mine?*

Did it have to happen this way?
Your playbill noted no intermission.
You drift away to a dear dead day,
forgetting, for a time, the cost of admission.

With neither light nor sense of time,
you wait there with the ache,
hoping to hear harmony and rhyme
rise like dawn and gently wake

your brave and battered heart.
You still dare to remain exposed—
not to reclaim a youthful start,
but to dance where something once was closed.

When the orchestra resumes in slower measure
and curtains lift with renewed grace,
you may hear a tune you used to treasure,
threaded through new time and space.

IV

Flicker and Smoke

IV.

Flicker and Smoke

There will be times when you don't feel ready to begin again, but you can sense something in you already whirring back to life.

There's a different kind of light here—where the flame hasn't returned, but memory casts a glow that makes your world look both real and surreal. And new lights may start to appear, even if only on the horizon.

Your steps shift gently as that light begins to return because beginnings don't always feel like beginnings. Sometimes, they arrive jagged, uncertain, or incomplete.

Even miracles are sharp when they come in fragments.

No one tells you that. People speak about miracles as if they arrive whole.

But so often, they don't.

They may hit you like the scent of a bakery carried on a morning breeze. And then you wander unfamiliar streets with rising hunger, searching for something you can't quite place.

Other times, they skip toward you at the sight of your face, only to slip suddenly out of view—too caught up in joy to notice the manhole cover in the path.

And still, we pay attention. Because even a flash of lightning is still light.

Here, longing softens from ache into curiosity, and what once burned hot now flickers in your hands, like a baby bird tentatively trying to fly for the first time.

Though it's not yet time to rise, this flicker means something wants to live—even if it doesn't burn clean yet.

Navigating this can feel confusing. You'll feel the weight of what could have been, the echoes of what still lingers, and the tentative pull of something not-yet-named beckoning you—sometimes all at once.

In the light smoke that still hangs in the air, you may catch yourself glimpsing the shapes of familiar faces—but not because you're meant to preserve them in a bottle or blow them back into formlessness.

For now, you can simply sit with the warmth that moves through you—unsteady but real. And know that even here, in the lingering smoke, the faintest flicker of something true is calling your name.

Prelude to Flicker

You don't have to name it.
Just notice what moves
when your hands remember warmth.

Flicker

There was a spark once.
Amber-soft,
a whisper on cold rain,
it flickered gently,
then went quiet.
It lived just long
enough to remind
a heart that it still kindles,
and to show hands
how to tend the hearth—
in case the next flame holds.

Prelude to Heavy Heart

Grief can be a wide, dragging weight
that smooths away your footprints
before you can name where you've been.
But even then, something in you
remembers how to keep walking.

Heavy Heart

When your heart feels heavy
with the weight of life's levy,
and you can't seem to let it go,

stop. Breathe. Remember what you know:
You've weathered
storms before when you felt tethered

to pain and despair.
No need to compare,
as no two hurts are quite the same,

but it can help to adjust the frame.
Feel the waves washing
over you without them squashing

your hopes and dreams and joys.
Cry. Scream. Make all the noise,
recalling the tide will recede,

and the thick fog will heed
the late morning sun, and clear.
Calmer, brighter days are near.

Prelude to What the Roots Remember

Sometimes, what we release
doesn't disappear.
It just seeps into the soil.

What the Roots Remember
(a convergence)

A path may bend where none could see,
drawn by time and soft gravity.
We carved our names into a tree
because what's lost may cease to be—
not by force but by setting free,
the roots remember patiently.
A silence held becomes a plea,
then breath, then song, then symphony.

Prelude to Heart Fell

*There's a kind of surrender
that doesn't settle anything.*

Heart Fell

Snagged in the space
between divine order
and careful chaos,

the temptation to chase
after daisy petals
long since yellowed
and blowing away—

a split surrender,
a letdown in letting go,
an existential crease
without true release.

Prelude to Six of Swords

Hope and fear may dance together in the moonlight.

Six of Swords

The last evening before, I checked the rope.
I adjusted my hands—felt the last of my hope
for our love—deeper yet, or not to be?
Thoughts, shapeless shadows, surrounded me...

When tomorrow arrives,
will we carry on with separate lives,
our bond breaking like dawn's first light—
or could we start anew and stay despite
the weight of warm words we once swore?

Might we burn through the burdens we bore?
Maybe our story was already told,
but still, I dreamed that we grew old.

Whether morning found us split
or our two hearts dazzlingly lit,
I wondered: *Must these paths drift wide—*
or could we choose to walk beside
who we are and who we need to be,
together, or each, individually?

But even if sunrise left us shattered,
I'd never question whether we mattered.

Prelude to Hourglass

Not every ending empties clean.
Some moments linger—
not to last,
just to be held
a little longer.

Hourglass

An hourglass etched with our names
ran out long ago—yet you and I are held transfixed.

What if we each placed a hand
upon it, fingers grazing gently, incidentally

but not, and together turned the hourglass
over? Could a sweet swan song that lingers

against all odds on hushed winter winds
give way to the resounding cries

of a baby phoenix in a cherry blossom nest?

Prelude to Fireflies

The night wasn't empty.
It was just quiet.

Fireflies

I thought love meant holding my breath,
standing polished and perfect
with my hands outstretched,
heart trembling, back aching,
at the edge of a crumbling bridge
again, so long after midnight,
hoping to be someone worth crossing for.
Finally, lungs full, I started singing
into lifetimes of silence,
my voice ricocheting off the cliffs,
splintering lifelong compliance.
Torches burst: a battalion of fireflies
in late spring, already lining the riverside,
illuminating wild blossoms
that had been growing quietly.

Prelude to Heart Sound

Some echoes don't fade.
They just change direction.

Heart Sound

I'm listening for what's listening for me, and I've checked
those quiet corners where memory clings,
like sonar seeking a ship long since wrecked.
I may not see what strikes my soul like plucked strings,
but I'll follow the cracked path lit by the waxing moon,
with an open chest and barefoot hope toward a rising tune.

Prelude to Right On Time

You may not know where you're going.
Only that you're the one choosing each step now.

Right On Time

A map is thrust into your hands as you leave
for an unwanted journey, thrust
into motion with no reprieve
by someone who held your trust.

Isn't it hard to read through tears that dot
the paper like fake lakes,
each a reminder to not
repeat past mistakes?

How do you feel about avoiding the main
roads and setting off through thick brush?
You'll leave footprints, heavy with pain,
but steady, with no need to rush

toward what's patiently waiting
with open arms as warm rain pours
down, out of sight, but creating
hopes of being always yours.

V

Becoming the Flame

V.

Becoming the Flame

There comes a moment—after the ache, after the ash—when you realize you're no longer just surviving.

It may sneak up on you, like an old friend with a warm smile, tapping you on the shoulder while you're focused on your work in a coffee shop.

But you won't be able to deny that something in you has taken root.

Not because the fire spared you but because it didn't—and you're still here.

What once broke you now lives in your voice and body.

Maybe you're not flying yet, but your wings are starting to stretch, even if they tremble.

Courage usually feels more like uncertainty than like what you imagine bravery feels like.

It may look like holding it together just enough to take the next step.

And doing it anyway.

It feels like showing up with your whole heart, even when shaking.

I'm reminded of a lyric from Australian singer-songwriter Gordi that has built a home inside me:

"I was always ready but unready for what this might do."

There's only so much you can learn and re-learn in lonely rooms.

Only so much of this healing work can be done in isolation.

Partly because we need others to help us write new stories on the blank pages we've turned to.

But also because even when you know you're ready to start writing something new, you won't know—you can't know—exactly what that will be.

Even after you've sifted through ruin and found something sacred buried in your own bones, you won't have certainty—no matter how much you long for a truth that offers freedom from future burns.

The next part is learning to let that be okay.

Prelude to Out of the Ashes

There will be small, ordinary moments
when you feel a strength or clarity
that's familiar but new,
like hearing a cover
of a favorite song that lands
in just the right way.

Out of the Ashes

They came without warning,
barefoot in the wreckage,
smelling faintly of lilies
and something like a campfire in rain.

You didn't glance up. Though if you had,
you still might not have recognized them.
How could you? Some things
only our bones can see.

But there they were,
brushing the ash from your shoulder,
gently placing your hand over your heart.

And when you wept,
they stayed.
They stayed.

And when you wiped
your eyes and did not see,
still, you knew:
this was your self
forged by fire.

The one
who made it
through.

Prelude to Ally

Sometimes, it's enough to just be there.

Ally

I wake in a room where I didn't fall asleep
to see you staring,
elsewhere, out the great window
at an old oak, lurching without its leaves,
stretching unsteadily over forgotten
acorns on a midnight lit, not by moon,
but a horizon glowing with a world aflame.
I call your name—softly. It sparks

no movement, absence aligned
with profound presence: we've
only met on the edge of what
could be. This shared space holds,
a sanctuary for a season
or a fort for a fortnight, where we muster
all we have to give a dying place.
We could stay here

a while longer,
before meeting a blaze whose reach widens
by the minute. What do we possess
that won't burn? Do we trust our kindled
hearts to warm those stripped
of blankets? I'd touch your hand

but for the fullness of what we
must choose to carry: words, wound
into weapons or woven to soothe wounds.
When desire dips to duty and boldness
bows to bearing, we nod toward futures
never written, powered by passion
yielded to purpose on fire's fringe.

Prelude to Unburied

Some burdens don't ask to be lifted—
only acknowledged as you pass through.

Unburied

these legs still
work, toiling,
climbing, climbing uphill,
inner heat rising, now near boiling,
heart loud
despite fatigue,
into the thick black cloud,
onward another league
toward joy, hope, and peace ...
oneness, connection, and ease—
out of sight, married to dread,
persistent but unhurried
after dreams, long dead,
yet unburied.

Prelude to Cathedral Heart

*Some spaces are built
not to be seen publicly,
but to be ready.*

Cathedral Heart

I dug up the broken cobblestones that cut my feet
for miles after my shoes surrendered.
Shoulders bowed, hands unwavering,
I massaged stone after stone into shape
with tears and almosts mixed into mortar.
I could have built a tomb. Instead, I constructed
a cathedral in my heart,
so that when the bells ring,
and love walks through the door,
it steps inside a place already made sacred.

Prelude to Saving a Life

It doesn't have to be dramatic
for it to be necessary.

Saving a Life

I fled the suffocating smoke,
bringing only what my hands, still bleeding
from the friction of an endless tug of war,
could hold: the scattered corners of myself
I had cut off over the years, cluttering
the floor but never swept away.
Maybe saving a life only feels heroic
looking backward, when you lift your face
to the open sky and fill your lungs
with air that's just yours.

Prelude to Indivisible

You don't have to become
someone else
to become whole.

Indivisible

Past and present cannot be split
apart, leaving me as I am,
all I am, however I fit,
or failed to, as I fought to cram

myself with all I had into someone
sadly unable to hold me gently.
Their shaping may never come undone.
Still, I'll show up for my task intently

and heal. I'm learning to love my own shape again
and steadily finding strength here in these scars.
There's been pain, true, but I've slipped the old chain,
and now I sing this new refrain among the stars.

Prelude to Vernacular

The shape of something
you almost know

Vernacular

There is much written about you
that you have yet to read. Today,
these words would still feel foreign
on your tongue. Someday,
they will sound like home.

Prelude to Broken (Open)

Sometimes, breaking open
is how the light gets in.
And how it finds its way out.

Broken (Open)

You disguise your fragility with a costume
of ignorance, as if wearing a paper mask
after everyone's left the grand ballroom
might render you invisible to your heart's task.

You long to rise like a brilliant yellow balloon
blazing on a blue sky, but self-doubt, a ballast,
keeps you grounded into a waning afternoon,
clutching a frayed rope, your exhausted hands calloused.

You hold your fear nearby and your wisdom apart.
But with tender care, tides turn and chasms close,
patience rewarded for your dawning work of art:
a golden sunrise over sunflower meadows.

Prelude to Not Yet

Arrival isn't always a destination.
It may just be the choice to keep going.

Not Yet

I stare down a path my eyes tell me I've walked before
but the pristine dirt reveals my eyes' lies.
I can see this same road covered by Frost
on a winter morning long ago, beckoning me

to follow my breath—wondering, wandering, lost
in thought, pondering whether or not to take it.

Flashes through my mind of times and people who live
only inside me now. I carry them with me everywhere, forever
forgetting they are ever there, never
growing unconscious to their weight.

Someday not too long from now, I hope
to find myself
at the end of this windswept road,
perhaps weary and worn but awoken,
perhaps teary and torn but aware of the unspoken
truth in the dirt that colors my shoes:

I went somewhere. I arrived.

Still, my legs
pulse, each spent muscle singing
into harmony a prayer:
Upward. Onward.
I stare down a path.

VI

Light That Stays

VI.

Light That Stays

In time, the fire settles. The ash cools. The smoke clears.

And you're left with a flame that's smaller but safer—one you no longer fear will burn down your home if you take your eyes off it for a second.

The tenderness you've always carried feels less like a question demanding an answer or a character flaw you can't fix.

Instead of being the overly dramatic friend who's sent you 14 texts since you started reading this page, your tenderness begins to resemble someone you might turn to for understanding or advice.

But remember: that person has needs and emotions too.

This isn't about becoming someone who no longer feels things deeply.

It's why this book is shaped like a spiral rather than laid out in a perfectly constructed linear fashion or organized by clear themes.

You keep feeling in the big, tender ways you always have. You just learn to hold it differently—to walk with yourself in a new way.

You'll still experience hard things, but they won't knock you over like they once did.

And it's not only about how you relate to challenges.

Sometimes, you'll feel something too beautiful to fully believe in without trembling first. You may feel the urge to grasp it too quickly—or to run, just to escape the open loop of possibility.

That's okay.

Those moments may tempt you to rush into false certainty, to choose a story you don't fully believe just because sitting with uncertainty feels too uncomfortable.

But maybe you need to linger in smaller rooms for a while—places where you can reach out and touch all four walls to steady yourself, where you can re-learn the sound of your own breathing when it isn't drowned out by shouts or wind.

Eventually, the future stops feeling urgent because the past has been gently woven into the fabric of who you are now.

We're not trying to reach some perfect end point.

But as we learn to stay with ourselves, we make space for the people and places that are meant to be here with us—however long they stay.

Prelude to Someone New

*You don't have to know what it is
for it to change you.*

Someone New

Someone new
is like camping overnight
on the mountain's peak
to watch the sun

rise the next morning.
A pink-hued tugboat
tows the sun, begrudgingly,

skyward. Will
clouds press their pillowy grip
or lose themselves
for hours

in peek-a-boo? Or perhaps
splatters from Van Gogh's brush
bathe you

in pigments
you can never wash out.

Prelude to Yellow Brick

You've been walking it all along.

Yellow Brick

Yellow bricks unfold ahead,
a golden path where I am led,
each block a moment to savor,
step by step, every subtle flavor.

Prelude to The Crucible

It got hot in here.

The Crucible

I think of diamonds
being put through all that pressure.
I wished that's what we were—
that pain would inevitably make us
beautiful, but it brought only opportunity:
a choice to sprout or sink,
shine or shrink,
and status quo—
just an illusion.

Prelude to Luna

The rhythm in your chest
may be the only map you need.

Luna

walking in the moonlight
trying to trust what feels right
can't give in to stage fright
might be out here all night

stepping over land mines
through veils of choking vines
finally paying old fines
searching for saving signs

striding down a moonbeam
letting out an ancient scream
wolves racing in my bloodstream
giving way to daydream

rooster ringing out in my ear
crows carrying off what I fear
recalling what I hold dear
that voice within is all I hear

Prelude to Songs of Samhain

On the thinnest night,
when the curtain slips loose, listen—
a note, not quite of this world,
rides the autumn wind,
signaling that those long gone
have taken up their instruments once more.

Songs of Samhain

Musicians with celestial score,
passing performers with holy hue
for an old opera, staged anew.
One night only. There can be no encore.

We sat spellbound in this long-lost space
with weeping woodwinds and shivering strings,
delighting in divas, as did kings,
the hours passed us by without a trace.

An aria under hunter's moon,
then the spectral orchestra sounding,
evoked a rapture so astounding,
before final bows that came far too soon.

For when darkness strayed, they could not stay,
but their melodies left lasting awe.
The fading stage fell silent. Into morning's maw,
they vanished through the gray.

Another year. We wait for this day.
Heaven's folly lets the veil waver,
bestowing us with dulcet favor,
when the light of life—briefly—gives way.

Prelude to Drumbeat

The music never stopped.

Drumbeat

Goodbye comes.
Neither the first nor
the last, but the drums
beat on, and the sands pour
through the crevice, as life hums,
rising behind it all, the shore
receives the wave, which becomes
the ocean once more.

About the Author

James Kerti is a poet and writer whose work explores self-trust, emotional resilience, and the way memory shapes us.

His debut collection, *Unfolding Love*, is a lantern-lit invitation for anyone learning to navigate the soft, uncertain places where love has left or changed shape.

In addition to writing poetry and prose, James works as an online business consultant for creatives and mission-driven organizations. His path has taken many unexpected turns, from basketball scouting to public service.

He lives in the Pacific Northwest.